WORLD OF READING

Dear Reader,

    This is your Reader's Journal to use as you read Garden Gates. It's full of good things for you to read, to look at, and to think about. You'll do things like pretend you are a frog on a mountain hike. You'll tell about a train trip to a special place. You'll make a prize for someone brave.

    If you think this sounds like fun, you are right. When you are done, this journal will be special, just like you.

Yours truly,
The Publisher

_____

Write your name here.

SILVER BURDETT & GINN

Needham, MA • Morristown, NJ • Atlanta, GA • Cincinnati, OH • Dallas, TX • Menlo Park, CA • Deerfield, IL

CONTENTS

UNIT 1 OPENING

Read the story to find out how Penrod does a "perfect" job.

Just Perfect

by Mary Blount Christian

Griswold had bought a pair of pants. He put them on. He turned around and around.

"Those pants are just perfect," Penrod said. "Almost."

"What do you mean, almost?" Griswold asked.

"They are a bit long," Penrod said. "But do not worry. I will fix them. Take them off."

Snip! Snip! Snip! Penrod cut the pants. Griswold put on the pants. "They are just perfect now," Penrod said. "Almost."

"Grrrrr!" Griswold said. "What is wrong with them?"

"Oh, nothing," Penrod said. "But your left leg is shorter than your right leg."

"Grrrrr!" Griswold said. "My legs are exactly the same length."

"Ummmm," Penrod said. "Then the left pant leg is longer than the right pant leg. Do not worry. I will fix it."

Snip! Snip! Snip! Penrod cut the left pant leg. Griswold put on the pants again. "Ummmm," Penrod said. "Now the right pant leg is longer than the left pant leg."

Snip! Snip! Snip! Penrod cut some more.

Griswold put on his pants. *"Grrrrr!"* he said. "Now both pant legs are the same. But they are too short for me!"

"But they are just perfect for me!" Penrod said.

UNIT 1

When Griswold's pants were too long, Penrod tried to fix them. He went *snip! Snip! Snip!*

This shirt is too long. What will you do to fix it? Write your plan.

_____

_____

_____

_____

_____

_____

Now the left sleeve is too short. What will you do to fix the shirt? Write your plan.

_____

_____

_____

_____

_____

Mountain Hike

Start at the bottom of this mountain. Make up something you saw at each flag . Did anything scare you? Were you brave? Write in your ideas.

I felt _____

_____

_____

At the top _____

_____

I felt _____

_____

Halfway up, I ran into a _____

_____

I felt _____

_____

At the bottom, I saw _____

_____

Start Here

◆ **DURING READING**

You are going to read about Frog and Toad. They climb a mountain to see if they are brave. Read to find out how brave they are.

A Card from Frog and Toad

Make a card from Frog and Toad. Draw a picture
on the front to show one thing that happened to
them on the mountain. Write a note to one of
their friends.

Front

Back

Dear _____

_____

_____

_____

_____

_____

Draw a stamp.

Post card

To:

_____

Pond Road
Water Way

An Island Trip

Pretend that Frog and Toad have just come back from a trip to an island. What did they see? What happened to them? Draw a picture of Frog and Toad on their island trip.

More

Now write a news story about what
Frog and Toad did on the island.

CONTENTS
page
36

Water Way News

Weather:
today sunny

Frog and Toad:
Island Hoppers Return!

_____

_____

_____

_____

_____

_____

_____

_____

_____

_____

What's Quacking?

Mother Duck has a nest full
of eggs. One of her eggs is
different. Draw her eggs.

Write what you think Mother
Duck says about her eggs.

_____

_____

_____

_____

_____

_____

_____

DURING READING   Read the next story, "The Ugly Duckling."
Find out how one duck was different.

Guess Who?

One day Swan visits his duck family. He is big now.
He looks different. Read the story. Make up an ending.

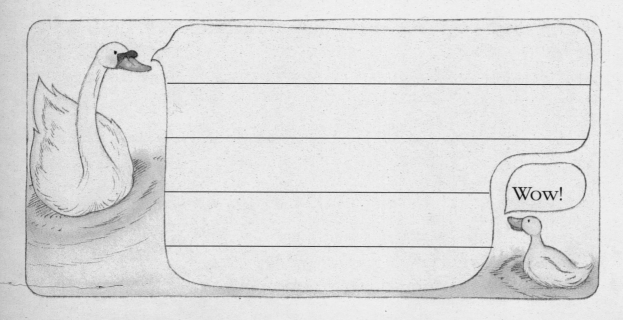

Show your ending to
someone in your class.

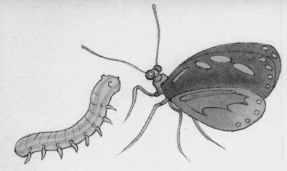

Changes

Many things change as they grow. A kitten grows into a cat. A duckling grows into a duck. The things pictured here will change as they grow. Draw how they could change. Can you think of another thing that changes? Draw a picture.

A seed   grows into

A girl   grows up to be

_____   grows into

More ▶

Write a story about one thing that grows up and changes. Take notes. Use the pictures on page 15 to help you.

Notes

How did the thing look at first? _____

_____

_____

How did the thing change? _____

_____

_____

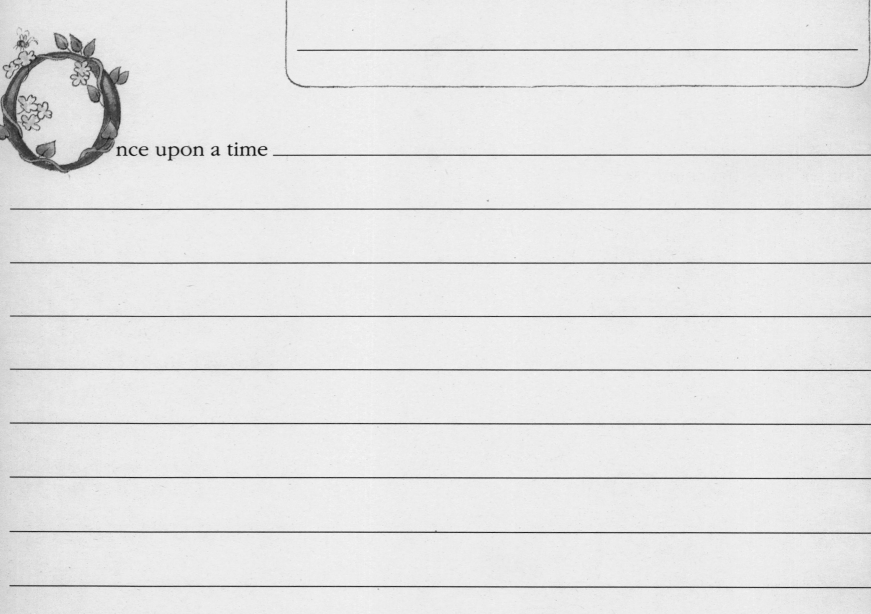

nce upon a time _____

_____

_____

_____

_____

_____

_____

_____

_____

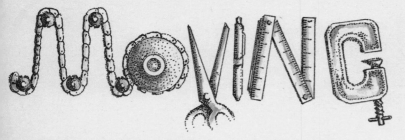

MOVING PARTS

Just about everything moves. The words on this page tell how things move. Draw a line from the picture to the word that tells about it. Then draw new pictures to go with *spin* and *run*.

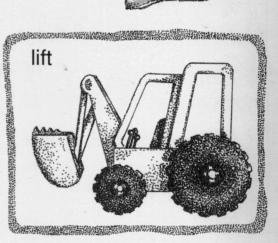

leap

spin

lift

run

DURING READING

The next story is called "Max." Max loves baseball. Find out how he learns some new moves.

What if Max told his team about dancing school? What would Max say?

Max would say _____

_____

_____

_____

_____

_____

What if Max told you about dancing school? What would you say?

_____

_____

_____

_____

_____

_____

_____

Dancers and Players

Baseball Players Practicing
Thomas Eakins, 1875

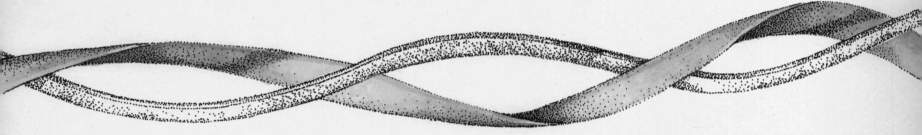

Dancers Practicing at the Bar
Edgar Degas, 1877

More ➤

Look at the pictures on page 19. Think about how dancing and playing baseball are the same. Think about how they are different. Write your ideas.

How are dancing and playing baseball the same?

_____

_____

_____

_____

_____

_____

How are dancing and playing baseball different?

_____

_____

_____

_____

_____

_____

Teachers Are All Around

We learn things all the time. Name some things
you have learned to do in the last year. Name the
teachers who helped you learn.

_____

_____

You learn things every place you go. Name some
places where you learn things.

_____

_____

DURING READING
The next story tells how one mother learned to
skate. Read to find out who her teacher was.

S T A R R Y
N I G H T

The next night, Makiko and her mother take Mr. Ogawa skating. Makiko is a good teacher. Her father learns fast. Soon the whole family is skating together. It is very cold, but skating keeps them warm. Pretend you are with the Ogawas. Tell what it is like to skate under the stars.

_____

_____

_____

_____

_____

_____

_____

HELP FOR HIRE

MAGIC LESSONS
Would you like to learn magic?
I can teach you.
Call Bill at 555-0000

JUMP ROPE
Jumping rope is fun!
I can teach you songs and show you special moves.
CALL LEE
555-0001

What kind of lesson would you like to give?
Make a sign. Use pictures and words.

More >

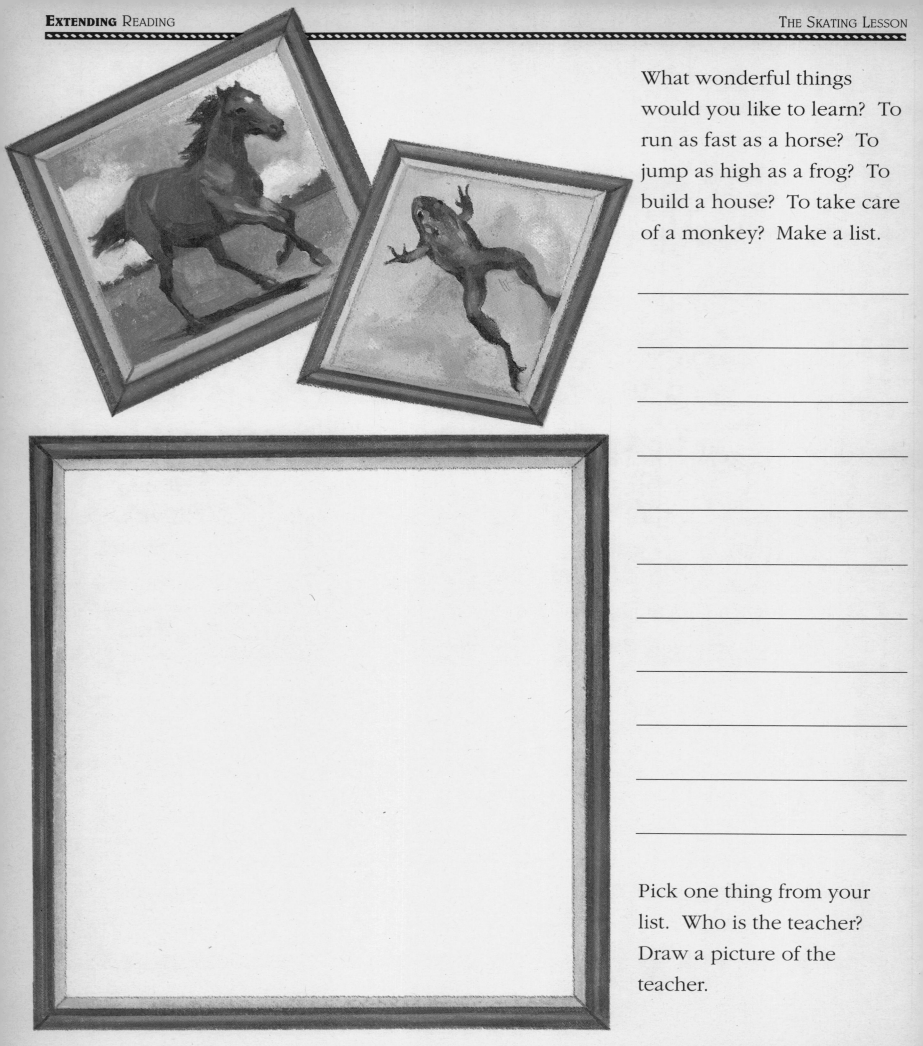

What wonderful things would you like to learn? To run as fast as a horse? To jump as high as a frog? To build a house? To take care of a monkey? Make a list.

_____

_____

_____

_____

_____

_____

_____

_____

_____

Pick one thing from your list. Who is the teacher? Draw a picture of the teacher.

Inside My Head Behind My Eyes

What do you see inside your head behind your eyes when you wish for something?

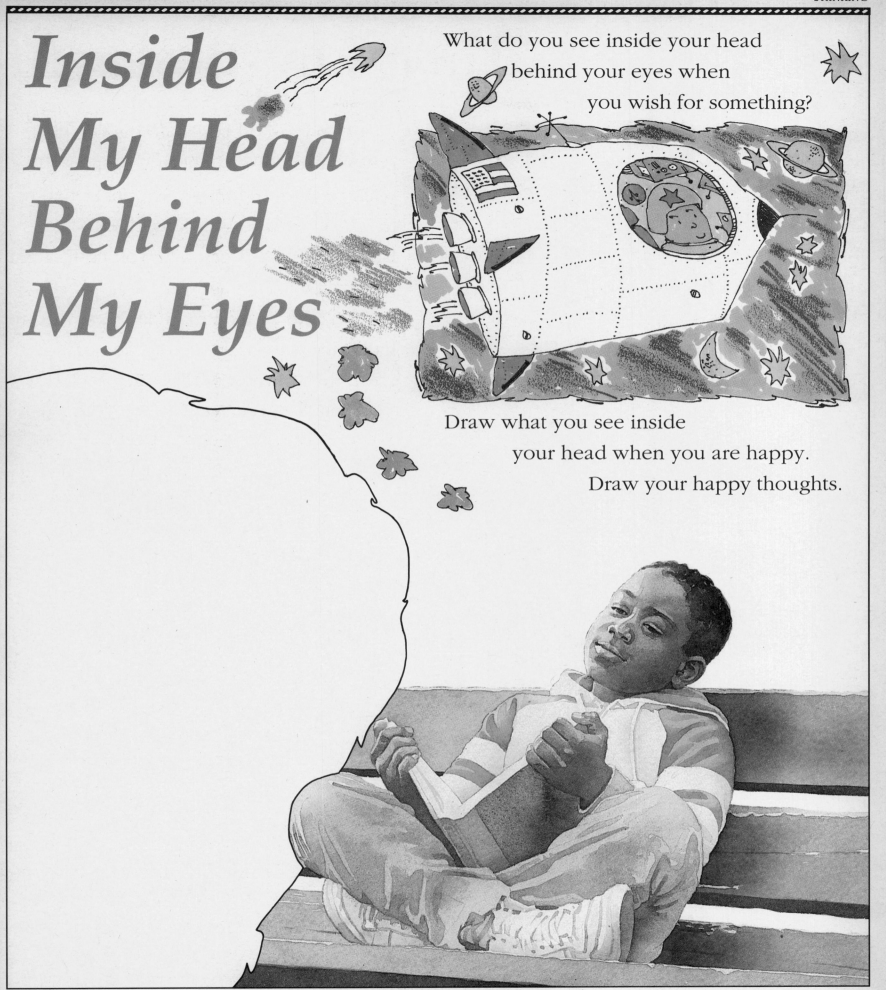

Draw what you see inside your head when you are happy. Draw your happy thoughts.

Turn On the Light

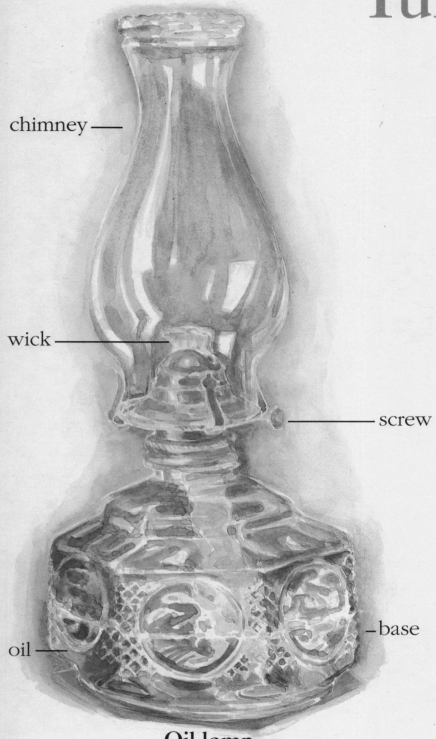

chimney —

wick —

screw

oil —

—base

Oil lamp

This is an oil lamp. In the old days, people used oil to light their homes. The wick was soaked in oil. A person had to turn the screw to lift the wick into the lamp chimney. Then a person could light the wick with a match.

To take care of an oil lamp, someone had to cut the wick. Someone had to clean the chimney. Someone had to fill the base with oil. Would you like to use an oil lamp today? Tell why or why not.

_____

_____

_____

_____

_____

_____

_____

_____

◆ **DURING READING**

In the next story, a girl named Abbie helps to light oil lamps. Read "Keep the Lights Burning, Abbie." Find out what her father learned from the burning lamps.

Dear Auntie

Pretend Abbie is writing a letter to her auntie about the week her father was away. Take notes. Finish the letter.

Notes
How did Abbie feel?

_____

_____

_____

Notes
What parts of her story did she write about?

_____

_____

_____

_____

Dear Auntie,

    Father sailed to town two weeks ago.

A storm started up.

_____

_____

_____

_____

_____

_____

_____

Love,

Abbie

Prizewinner

Draw a picture of Abbie doing one brave thing.

List other brave things she did.

_____

_____

_____

Put a star by the bravest thing she did.

If you lived on Matinicus Island, you might want
to give Abbie a prize. Draw the prize.

Tell what each person might say about Abbie's prize.

Papa _____

_____

Mama _____

_____

Lydia _____   Show your prize picture to
                                                           a friend. Find out if your
_____   friend ever won a prize.

Color in the face that shows how much you liked each story, article, or poem in this unit.

Frog and Toad

The Ugly Duckling

Max

The Skating Lesson

Thinking

Keep the Lights Burning, Abbie

Draw a line under the name of your favorite story, article, or poem. Circle the one you liked least.

On what page in your Reader's Journal do you think you did your best work for this unit? Why do you think so?

30

Choose what you want to do.

Brave People
Draw and cut out pictures
of people doing brave things.
Make a "Brave People" sign for
your classroom.

Feathered Friends
Read about ducks
and swans. Write
a paper about how
they are different.

FIRE STATION
Visit a fire station. Ask the firefighters
about brave things they have done.
Take notes. Write about your trip.

CITY MOUSE –
COUNTRY MOUSE

by Aesop • Pictures by Marian Parry

What do you like about the city? What is nice about country life? As you read this story, think about where you would rather live.

Once upon a time a City Mouse went to visit his cousin in the country.

The Country Mouse was happy to see his cousin.

The Country Mouse did not have fine food, but he was happy to share what he had with the City Mouse.

The City Mouse turned up his nose at the country food. And he invited his cousin to have dinner with him in the city.

No sooner said than done. The two mice set off for the city.

At last they came to the home of the City Mouse. It was very late at night.

The City Mouse led the Country Mouse right into

a grand dining room. The leftovers of a fine feast were still on the table.

Soon the two mice were eating jam and cake and all that was nice.

Suddenly they heard growling and barking.

All at once the door flew open, and in came two huge dogs. Both mice ran for their lives.

The Country Mouse made up his mind to go back to the country that very night.

What good is fine food if you can't enjoy it! It is much better to eat plain food in peace.

UNIT 2

Which would you choose to be, a city mouse or a country mouse? Fill in what the mice might say about city life and country life. Then write your choice.

The life of a city mouse
is best because

_____

_____

Oh, no! It is better to be a
country mouse because

_____

_____

And that's not all! Another reason is

_____

_____

But what about

_____

_____

I would choose to be a _____ **mouse because** _____

_____

_____

_____

Come Right In

What is a home? Read what some people have said about a home.

Make a sign to tell what a home is to you. Use pictures and words.

DURING READING

Read the next story, "My House." Find out why one girl thinks of her home as a friend.

A Friendly House

The girl in the story said, "When a house is your house, you get to know it like a friend." How can a house be like a good friend? Read the girl's idea. Then add your own.

Grows older with you

Draw a picture of you and a friend at your house. It can be inside or outside. It can be your real house or a pretend one.

Home Pictures

Pretend the girl from "My House" is making
a book of family pictures. You can help.
Write about each picture to finish this page.

Mom dropped
the spaghetti.

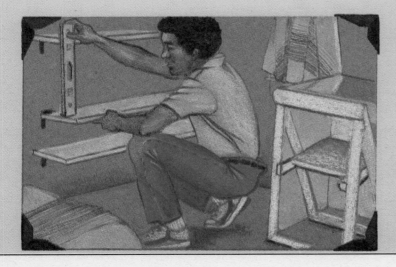

More

Draw some family pictures. They can be pictures of your real family or the family of the girl from the story. Write what they are about.

Write a story to tell about one picture on this page.

Tiny House

There was an old woman
Who lived in a shoe.
She had so many children,
She didn't know what to do.

What is nice about living in a tiny place
with many brothers and sisters?

_____

_____

_____

_____

_____

What is hard about it?

_____

_____

_____

_____

_____

DURING READING

Read the next story, "Not So Wise As You
Suppose." Find out what the farmer learns that
makes him feel better about his little house.

House Rules

How can the farmer's family keep from bumping into each other? How can they keep from talking at the same time? The farmer's family is writing some rules. Help them finish the rules.

Rules for Walking

Rules for Talking

Read your rules to someone in your class. Have a friend read his or her rules to you. Talk about which rules will work best.

MANY HOUSES in ONE

Pretend that the farmer went to the city to look at some apartment buildings. Read the note he wrote to his family.
Look at the picture.

My dear family,
  Let's think about moving to the city. We could live in an apartment building. Do you think you would like to? Many families have homes inside. Would you mind leaving the farm?   Love,
                                Dad

More →

How do you think the
farmer's family will answer
him? Will they want to live
in an apartment building?
Will they want to stay on the
farm? Write the farmer a
letter that tells his family's
answer.

Dear Dad,

_____

_____

_____

_____

_____

_____

_____

_____

_____

_____

Love,
The family

Let's Face It

Do these houses make you think of
anyone? Give each house a name.

Draw your own face house.
Give it a name.

Just Smile and Say Hello

Did you ever feel lonesome? What did you do to cheer yourself up? Draw a picture of you doing something to cheer yourself up.

Write one other thing you do to cheer yourself up.

_____

_____

_____

 **DURING** READING

Read "Howdy!" Find out what a boy named Luke did to cheer up a whole neighborhood.

HATS
OFF
TO YOU

Luke wore a cowboy hat and said, "Howdy!"
He made people happy. Draw your own
good neighbor hat. Write what you would
say to your neighbors.

Luke's Neighborhood

Use a pencil to follow the sidewalk
from Luke's apartment to the school.
Read each sign.

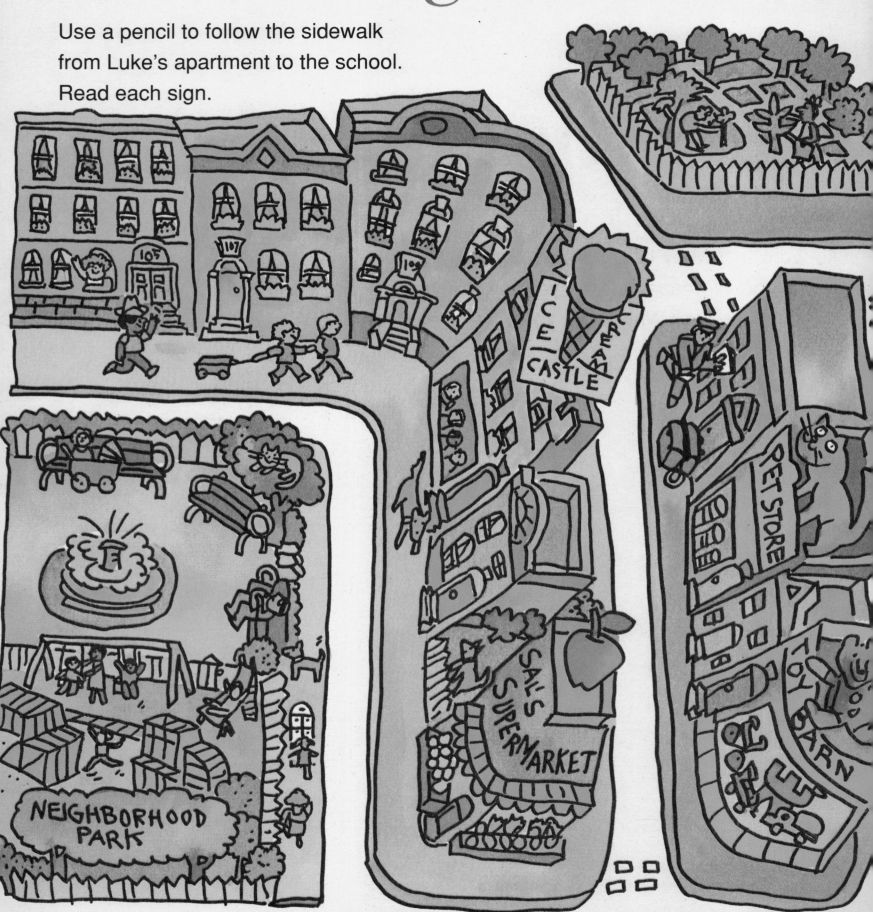

Write about what might have
happened as Luke went to school.

_____

_____

_____

_____

_____

_____

_____

_____

_____

A Place to Eat and Sleep

Houses come in many shapes, sizes, and colors. Read the poem.

Some houses stand tall.
Some sit small.
Some are shaped like cones.
Others are made of stones.
Some are not so long.
Some are big and strong.
What kind of house would you like?

Would you like a red house that's thin?
Or a shiny one made of tin?
Would you like a blue house made of glass?
Or a little green one made of grass?
Would you like a house with towers?
Or one with lots of flowers?
What kind of house would you like?

Write about the kind of house you would like.

_____

_____

_____

_____

_____

_____

 DURING READING

Read "Pueblos of the Southwest." Find out about a special kind of house called a pueblo.

FROM THE EARTH

Pretend you are a Pueblo man or woman. Tell what you might do with the things on this page.

stones
and
mud

_____

_____

_____

branches
and
grasses

_____

_____

_____

_____

feathers

_____

_____

grinding
stone

_____

_____

_____

TO SEE and TO USE

Here are some pictures of Pueblo pots. Pueblo pots have shapes and lines. Some pots have animal pictures on them.

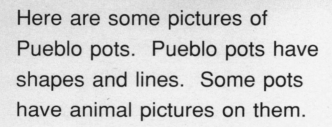

Make your own clay pot. Draw animals,
lines, or shapes on it. The pictures can be
your own, or they can look like lines and
shapes from a Pueblo pot.

Inside Out

Think about the inside of your home.
What are some things you see in the
different rooms?

What do you see in a bedroom?

_____

_____

_____

_____

What do you see in the kitchen?

_____

_____

_____

_____

_____

_____

What do you see in the living room?

_____

_____

_____

 DURING READING

You are going to read a poem called "My
Pueblo Home." As you read it, try to picture
the inside of a Pueblo home.

At Home

"My Pueblo Home" tells about things that
people do in a Pueblo village. Here are
some of those things:

making adobe bricks
plastering walls with brown clay
sitting by the fireplace
grinding corn

Draw a picture of you in a Pueblo village
doing one of these things.

Dreams

Pueblo Dreams
Tommy Edward Montoya

This is a painting by a Pueblo artist, Tommy Montoya. He called it *Pueblo Dreams*. Why do you think he gave it that name?

Think of a place you like. It can be in the city
or in the country. It can be a place you see
from a window or from a hill. It
can be real or pretend. Draw
your place. Then write about
it – where it is, why you like it,
when it is nicest.

My special place _____

_____

_____

_____

_____

_____

_____

_____

Share your picture with a friend. Tell your friend
what you like best about your special place.

Color in the face that shows how much you liked each story, article, or poem in this unit.

Draw a line under the name of your favorite story, article, or poem. Circle the one you liked least.

My House

Not So Wise As You Suppose

Houses

Howdy!

Pueblos of the Southwest

My Pueblo Home

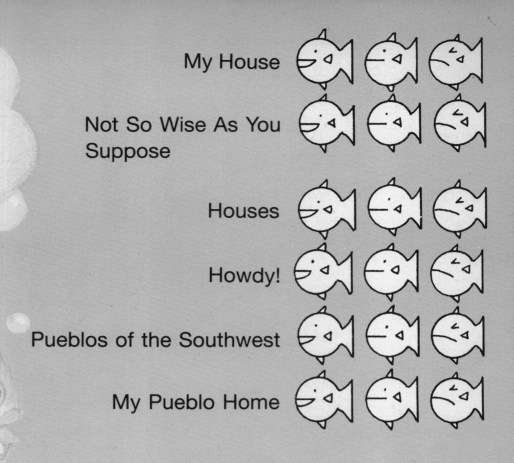

On what page in your Reader's Journal do you think you did your best work for this unit? Why do you think so?

Choose what you want to do.

Space Place
Pretend you are someone from another planet, like E.T. Write about what your home is like. Draw a picture.

Other Words
Learn how to say "our house" in French and Spanish.

Other Lands
At the library, learn how children live in Mexico, China, Russia, Kenya, or India.

Indian Homes
Read about another kind of American Indian home: a wigwam, a teepee, or a hogan. Draw a picture.

Welcome
Make a "Welcome to Our School" book. Draw and write about the children and teachers. Your book could have a map, too.

UNIT
3
OPENING

As you read the poems
on these pages, think about
things that are treasures to you.

HAIRY JONES

by Kathleen Hague

Hairy Jones, Brittany's bear,
Was furry to the touch.
His eyes are gone.
His tummy's wrong.
He's been hugged and loved so much.

The Park

by James S. Tippett

I'm glad that I
    Live near a park

For in the winter
    After dark

The park lights shine
    As bright and still

As dandelions
    On a hill.

KEEPSAKES

by Leland B. Jacobs

I keep bottle caps,
    I keep strings,
I keep keys and corks
    And all such things.

When people say,
"What good are they?"
The answer's hard to get
For just how I will use them all
I don't know yet.

UNIT
3

Name some old treasures.

_____

_____

_____

Name some new treasures.

_____

_____

_____

Name some treasures you see in the country.

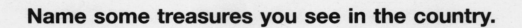

_____

_____

_____

Name some treasures you see in the city.

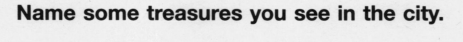

_____

_____

_____

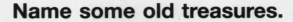

Looking Back

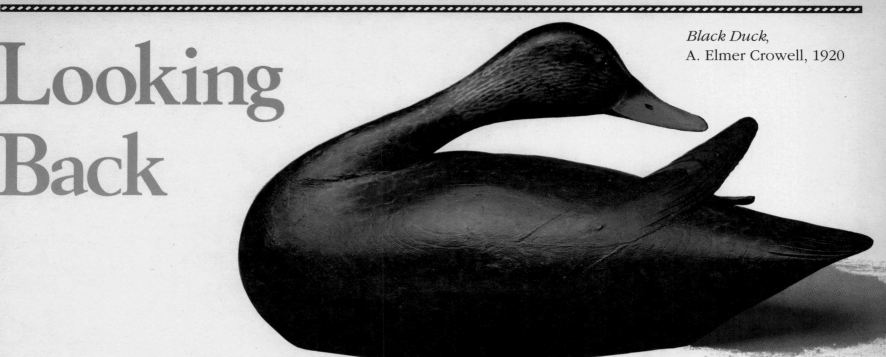

Black Duck,
A. Elmer Crowell, 1920

Look at the carved duck by A. Elmer Crowell. Why do you think the artist carved it with its head facing its wing?

_____

_____

_____

Do you think this makes the carving more fun to look at? Why?

_____

_____

_____

Have you ever seen live ducks? Where did you see them? What were they doing?

_____

_____

_____

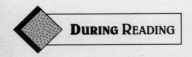 **DURING READING**   Read the next story, "Daniel's Duck." Find out why Daniel carved his duck the way he did.

Story Quilt

Daniel's mother made a quilt for the fair.
A quilt is a kind of blanket. It is made of
pieces of cloth. A quilt maker sews the
pieces together to make pictures.
Make a story quilt. On each square of
the quilt, draw a picture that tells part of
the story "Daniel's Duck."

Henry Pettigrew's House

Pretend that you are Daniel. Then pretend that you visit Henry Pettigrew's house after the fair. What do you see? What do you learn? Write some notes.

NOTES
What did I see?

_____

_____

_____

_____

_____

_____

NOTES
What did I learn?

_____

_____

_____

_____

_____

_____

More >

Now write in Daniel's diary about the visit.
Use your notes. Write some things you saw
and learned.

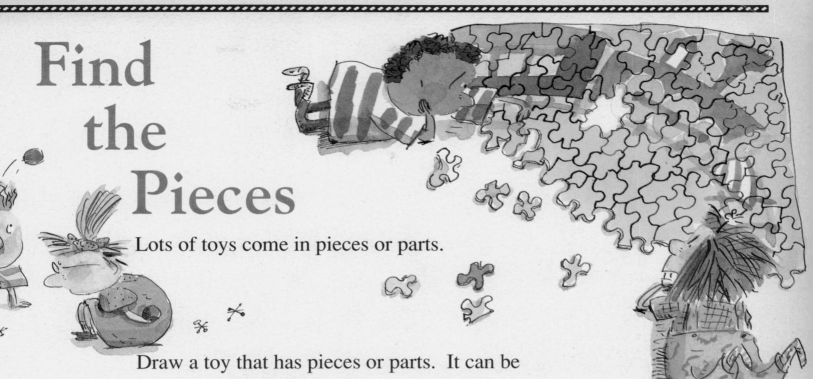

Find the Pieces

Lots of toys come in pieces or parts.

Draw a toy that has pieces or parts. It can be
a real toy. Or it can be a toy you make up.

DURING READING Read the next story, "The Train Set." Find out how
many gifts a boy named Peter gets for his birthday.

Thank You

Can you think of something you want very much—the way Peter wanted the train set? Pretend that someone gives you the gift you want. Make a thank-you card to show how much you like the gift. Draw a picture on the front of the card. Then write the note.

front

Dear_____,

_____

_____

_____

_____

_____

Love,

_____

inside

A Train Trip

What if Peter got to go on a real train trip for his next birthday? Draw a picture of what he might see through the window of the train. Then write about your picture.

More

Where might Peter go on his train trip? It can be a real place or a make-believe place. Draw a picture of the place. Write about something that Peter might do in this new place.

Tell a friend about a trip you took. It can be real or make believe. Listen to your friend's story.

Who, What, When, Where, Why, How?

If you could talk to one special person, who would it be? A writer? An artist? A ballplayer? A racer? Someone else? What questions would you ask? Write the person's name and four questions.

A TALK WITH

_____

Question 1 _____

_____

Question 2 _____

_____

Question 3 _____

_____

Question 4 _____

_____

 **DURING READING**

Read the interview with Aliki. Does she answer any of the questions you wanted to ask in your interview?

LISTEN TO THE MUSIC

Drawing is Aliki's favorite thing to do. But music helps her to do her work. What are some things that you like to do to music? Dance? Do magic tricks? Clean up? Fix things? Write some things you like to do to music. Then write how the music makes you feel while you are working.

Things I like to do to music

How the music makes me feel

An Artist's Job

When Aliki was a child, she drew a picture of Peter Rabbit's family. Pretend you are a children's book artist. Draw a picture of your favorite story animal or person.

Name of story _____

More Fruit

Fruits grow on many different kinds of plants and trees. Draw the fruits in each picture.

Draw the peaches on the peach tree.

Draw the grapes on the grapevine.

Draw the oranges on the orange tree.

Draw the bananas on the banana plant.

Draw the berries in the berry patch.

Draw the apples on the apple tree.

 DURING READING

Read "The Story of Johnny Appleseed." Find out how Johnny's seeds grew and changed America.

Johnny's Friend

Johnny Appleseed made many friends while planting apple seeds. Pretend that you are one of Johnny's friends—a pioneer, a forest animal, or an Indian. Write about your visit with Johnny.

Let a friend read about your visit with Johnny.

My Hero

Johnny Appleseed was a folk hero. A folk hero is someone who is remembered for doing great things. Johnny Appleseed was a real person. But many folk heroes were made up. Read about some make-believe folk heroes.

Paul Bunyan was so big and so strong he could pull a tree out of the ground. He could dig a river by himself—or chop up a giant tree quicker than you can say "Johnny Appleseed." And could he eat? No one's ever downed a bigger load of pancakes.

Paul Bunyan with his friend, Babe the Blue Ox

Pecos Bill with his horse, Widow-Maker

Pecos Bill was as hard as nails. He grew up with a pack of wild coyotes. He could ride a mountain lion or fight a bear. Once he grabbed lightning from a storm cloud—to make it rain.

Pretend that Johnny Appleseed met one of these make-believe folk heroes. Who was it? Write his name.

_____

Pretend that they became good friends. But one day they had to move to different places. What good-by gifts did they give each other? Draw a picture of each gift. Then write what it was.

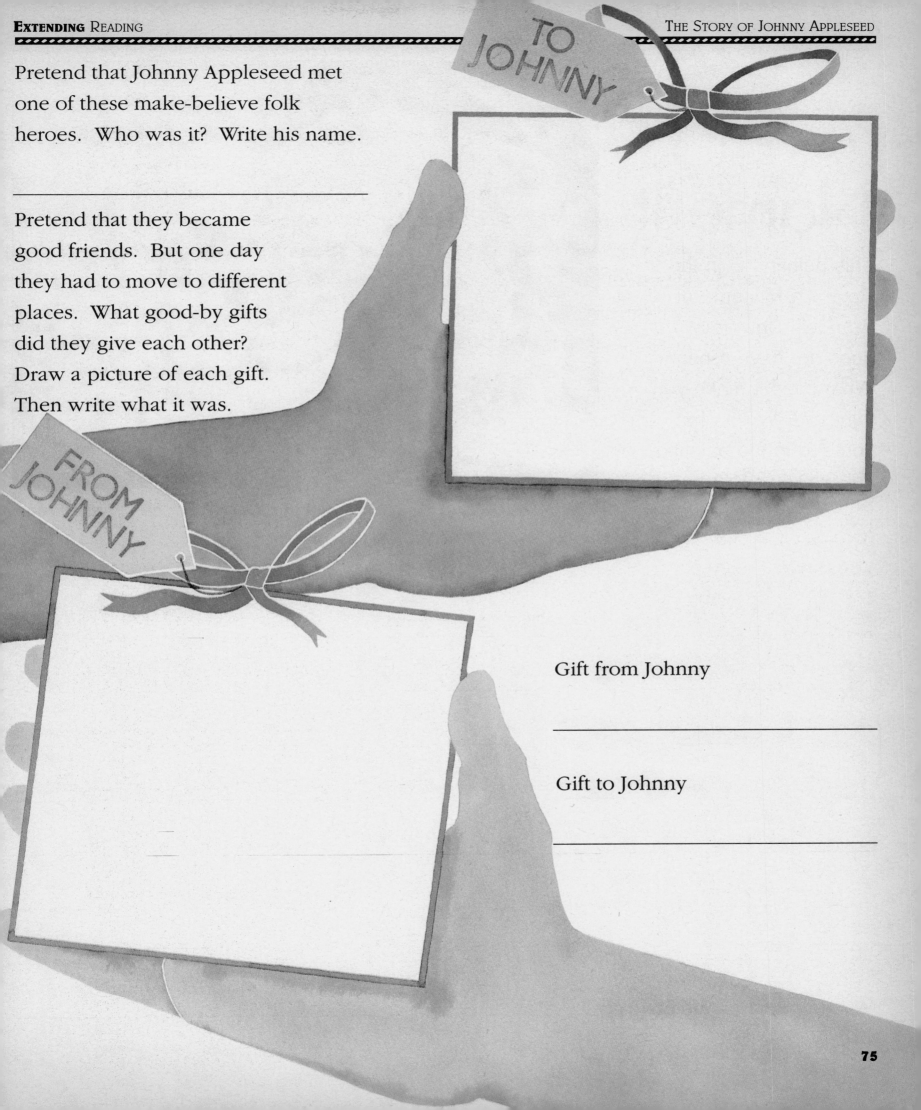

Gift from Johnny

_____

Gift to Johnny

_____

Name It

This painting is in the
Rose Art Museum at
Brandeis University. It
does not have a name.
What does it make you
think of? Write what
you see in the painting.
Tell why.

Untitled, Lee Krasner, 1938,   Rose Art Museum, Brandeis University, Gift of Mr. Samuel Shapiro, Swampscott, Massachusetts

_____

_____

_____

_____

_____

_____

_____

_____

Write a name for the painting. _____

Pick One

There are many kinds of museums. Here are some things you might see in different museums.

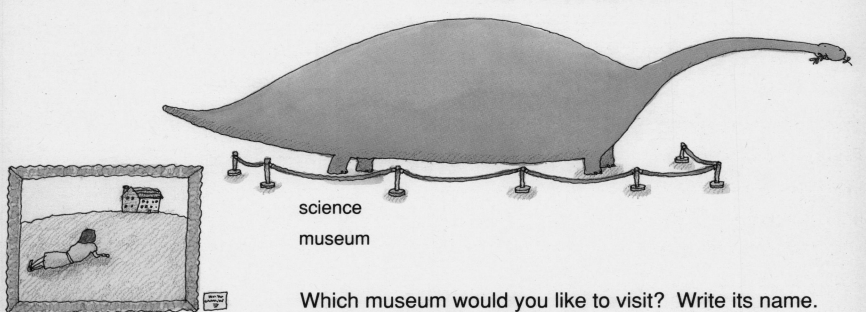

science museum

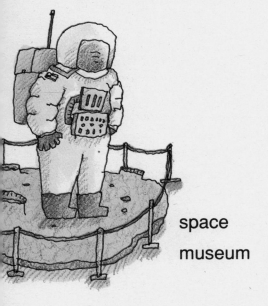

art museum

space museum

Which museum would you like to visit? Write its name.

_____

Tell why you would like to visit that museum.

_____

_____

_____

_____

_____

sports museum

 DURING READING

Read "The Smithsonian Institution." Find out how the Smithsonian is a special kind of museum.

More Treasures

Museums are like treasure chests. What treasures would you like to see from the Smithsonian? Fill the chest with one or more pictures of things you would like to see. Then write what is in your treasure chest.

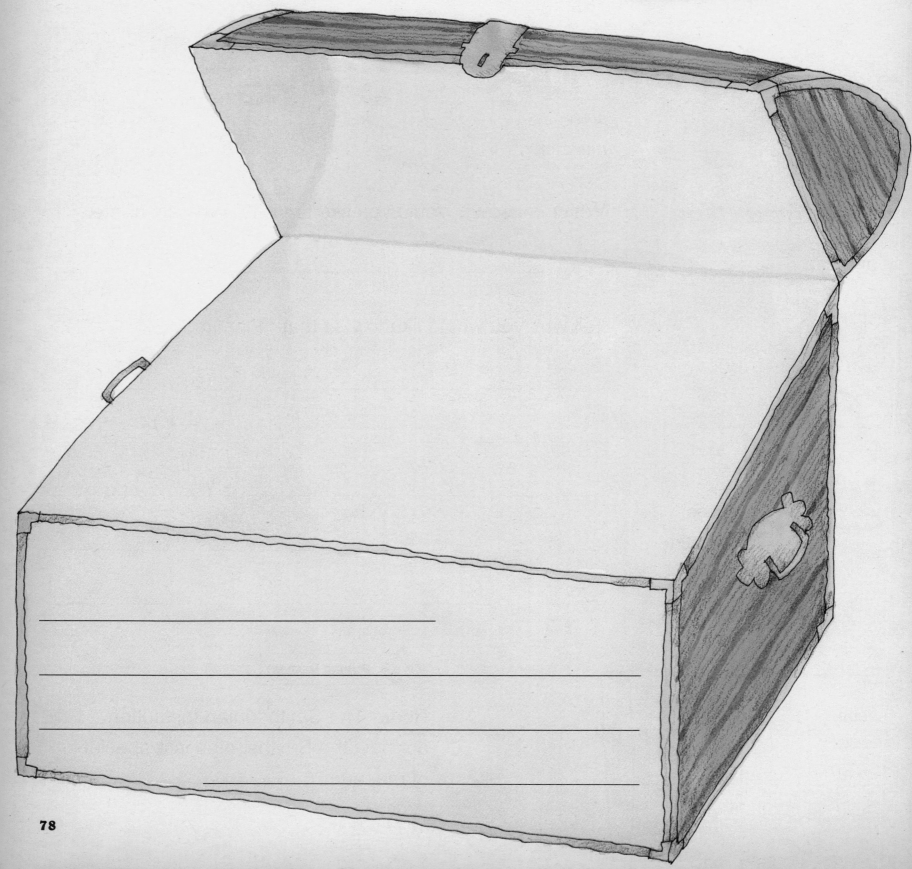

Our Place

Many cities have children's museums—special museums for young people. They are filled with rooms of fun things to see and do. On this page, circle the names of things you would like to find in a children's museum.

bone room

doll's house

dress-up room

bubble room

animal farm

climbing spaces

big town

More ➤

What if you had a chance to build one room in a
children's museum? What would it look like?
What would you put in it? Use the pictures on
page 79 to give you ideas. Write your name on
the line. Then draw a picture of your fun room in
the children's museum.

_____ 's Fun Room

Color in the face that shows how much you liked each story, article, or poem in this unit.

Draw a line under the name of your favorite story, article, or poem. Circle the one you liked least.

Daniel's Duck

The Train Set

Lee Bennett Hopkins Interviews Aliki

The Story of Johnny Appleseed

The Museum

The Smithsonian Institution

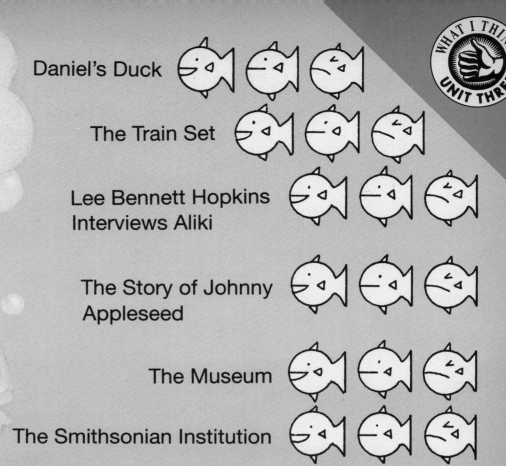

Write why you liked your favorite story, article, or poem.

More

81

Write the name of the story person or story animal you liked best. Tell why.

Spend a few minutes looking over the work you did in your *Reader's Journal* for this unit. On what page do you think you did your best work? Why do you think so?

Choose what you want to do.

Our Fair

With your class, plan a fair. Make things to show at it, like paintings and masks. Or show your favorite treasure. Write signs to tell about each thing and whose it is.

ANIMAL MOBILE

Make a mobile. Color and cut out five animal shapes. Find a stick about as long as two rulers. Cut six pieces of string, some longer than others. Tape the end of one string to the top of each animal. Tie the other end to the stick. Tie the last string to the middle of the stick. Hang your mobile from this string.

I Was There

Visit a museum in your town. Write a letter to a friend about what you saw. Draw a picture of you at the museum. Mail your letter and the picture to your friend.

Tree Treasures

Find out about one of the world's biggest treasures, the Amazon Rain Forest. Learn why trees are important.

83

THE WINTER PICNIC

by Robert Welber

In this story, a boy named Adam wants to have a picnic. It's snowing outside, but Adam has a plan. Read to find out if his plan works.

When it began to snow again Adam went to tell his mother he wanted to go on a picnic.

"Oh no," she said. "You don't go on picnics in the winter. It's too cold."

"I want to have a picnic," Adam said.

"When it's warm and sunny we'll have a picnic. When summer comes we'll go to the beach and have a picnic," his mother told him.

"Is that a long time?"

"Yes, a long, long time. In winter you can play in the snow. Why don't you go play in the snow?"

Adam went outside in the snow. He played he was sitting and having a picnic. He made plates out of the snow. He made cups out of the snow. He made a bowl out of the snow. Then he went to find his mother. "I'm having a picnic," he said to her.

"Are you? I'm cleaning this closet."

"I'm going to make some sandwiches," he said.

"Fine. Just let me finish what I'm doing," his mother said.

He went to the kitchen and took the bread out. He made peanut butter and boysenberry jelly sandwiches. He made lemonade with a fresh lemon and water and sugar. He took some potato chips out of the box. Then he went to find his mother. She was still cleaning the closet. "I made some peanut butter sandwiches for the picnic," he said.

"I'm glad."

"Would you like some?"

"Adam, please! Can't I be allowed to finish one thing I start. Just once. That's all I ask. Just once!"

Adam went back to the kitchen and put everything he had made into a big red pan and took it outside in the snow. It had stopped snowing, but it was very cold. He put the sandwiches on the snow plates. He poured the lemonade into the snow cups. He put the potato chips in the snow bowl. Then he went to find his mother. "Will you have a picnic with me?" he asked.

She sighed. "Out in the snow?"

"Yes," he said.

He took her hand and pulled her outside in the snow. When she saw the peanut butter and boysenberry jelly sandwiches on the snow plates and the lemonade in the snow cups and the potato chips in the snow bowl, she was very, very silent.

"I was wrong," his mother said. "You can have a picnic in winter." And she laughed.

They sat down and began to eat their winter picnic together.

UNIT
4

Now draw a picture of a picnic basket for a winter picnic.
Write about the picnic basket.
Tell what foods you would like to put inside your winter picnic basket.

_____

_____

_____

_____

_____

_____

What's Cooking?

Many cooked foods are made from more than one thing. Think about soups, breads, and pies. Choose one cooked food you like to eat. Draw a picture of it in a dish.

Write a list of the things that are in the food you have drawn. If you aren't sure, make them up.

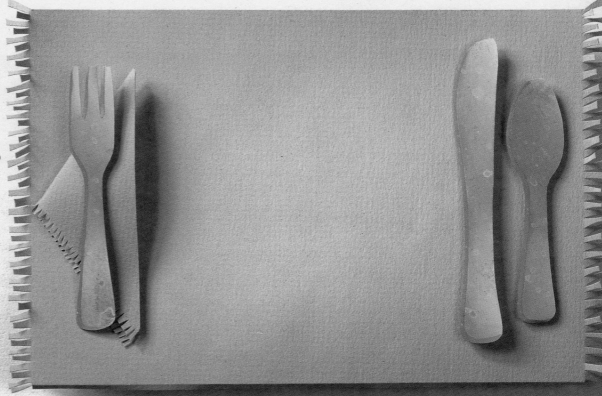

Now tell how to make your food.

_____

_____

_____

_____

_____

_____

_____

Read the next story, "Too Many Babas." See what happens on a cold day when four people try to cook one pot of hot soup.

DURING READING

Too Many Helpers

When all the Babas put things into the soup, the soup becomes too strong. It tastes terrible! Funny things sometimes happen when too many people try to help. Look at these pictures. Read the words below them. Think of a funny thing that could happen if too many people tried to help do each thing. Then finish each picture. Color or draw what could happen.

Too many people painted one wall.

Too many people wrote the words on one box to mail.

Too many people built one doghouse.

Let's Work Together

The Babas learned that when people work together, it's good for everyone to have a special job. Pretend that you and some friends are having a birthday party for another friend. Your special job is to plan the party. First, invite people to the party. Write and draw on a card to send them.

A Birthday Party for

_____

Where: _____

When: _____

Write what you want to eat and drink.

_____   _____

_____   _____

Write the games you will play.

_____   _____

More ➡

Draw a picture of your friends having fun at the party you have planned. Show the food. Show the games. Show the birthday person. If you plan to have hats and balloons at the party, show them, too.

Helping Hands

The poem "Helping" tells about two kinds of help. Look at this painting by Norman Rockwell. In it, a boy scout is helping a cub scout tie a special knot. Which kind of helping does the painting show, the kind "we all can do without," or the kind "that helping's all about"? Write your answer. Then tell why you think so.

A Guiding Hand, Norman Rockwell, 1946

_____

_____

_____

_____

_____

Think of a time when someone really helped you. Write about it.

_____

_____

_____

_____

A Place for a Book

Libraries have many different kinds of books. Librarians put each kind in a place so people can find them. Here are some of the stories, poems, and articles you have read. Read the names. Then help the librarian. Write each name in the list where it belongs.

Pueblos of the Southwest

Daniel's Duck

Too Many Babas

My PUEBLO Home

The Museum

FROG AND TOAD

The Smithsonian Institution

The Ugly Duckling

Stories About Animals   Stories About People

_____   _____

_____   _____

Articles About Places   Poems

_____   _____

_____   _____

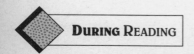 DURING READING

Read "Check It Out." Find out more about libraries.

BOOK FUN

Here are the names of some people and an animal you have read about in your book.

Max

Daniel

Makiko

Abbie

Johnny Appleseed

The Ugly Duckling

If you could be one of them, who would you like to be? _____

Write two sentences to tell why you would like to be this person or animal.

_____

_____

_____

_____

ow draw
picture of yourself
oing something this person or animal would do.

MY LIBRARY

Pretend you are making a library just for yourself and your friends. What will you name it? Write the name on the line.

Now fill your library with your favorite books. Maybe you want to have books about animals, games, toys, and famous people. Maybe you want to have fairy tales or stories about people your age. Write the book names on the book covers. Use real names or make them up.

Now that you have books in your library, what else will you have in it? Maybe you want to have a fish tank, so you can study fish. Maybe you want some paintings on the walls. Maybe you want a space for listening to music or a storytelling corner. Draw a picture of your library. Show yourself and some friends doing the things you have chosen.

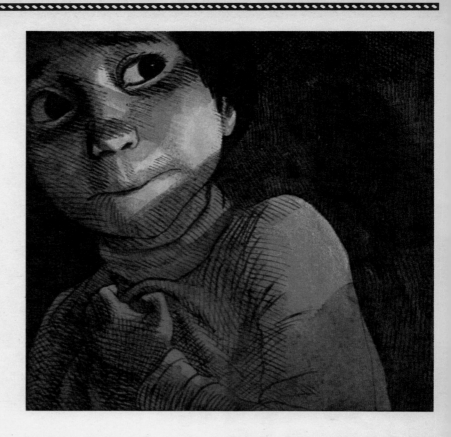

Remember?

Can you remember the first time you went to school? Or the first time you lost a tooth? Or the first time you were in a play at school? Write some "first times."

Pick one of your "first times." Write about how you felt.

_____

_____

_____

_____

_____

_____

Write about what happened during one of your "first times."

_____

_____

_____

DURING READING

Read "Nick Joins In." Find out what things a boy named Nick does for the first time.

Nick's New Friend

After school, Timmy talked with Nick.
Write what you think Nick said.

Timmy: How did you like your first day at school?

Nick: I had a good day. It was much better than I thought it would be.

Timmy: What did you like best today?

Nick: _____

_____

_____

Timmy: What was the hardest thing you did today?

Nick: _____

_____

_____

Timmy: I'm glad you are my new friend.

Nick: _____

_____

_____

Welcome Club

Pretend that your school has a Welcome Club. The club gives each new child a welcome basket. Inside the basket is a school map, a list of teachers, and some pencils. This basket is for Nick. Can you think of any other things that might make him feel welcome? Draw those things in the basket.

Write some things you could do to make Nick feel welcome.

_____

_____

_____

_____

Draw a picture of you doing one thing to welcome Nick.

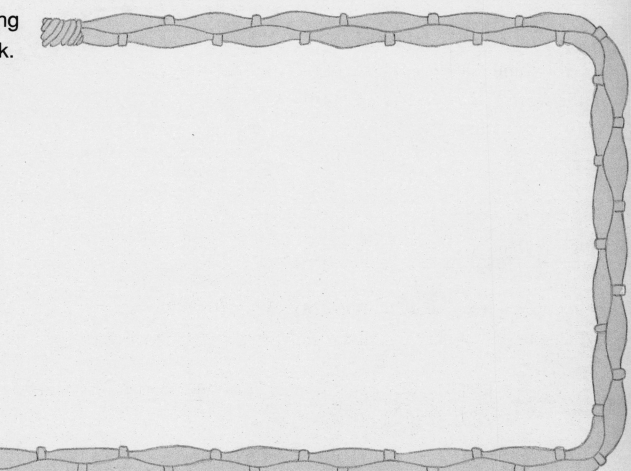

What would you like someone to do for you to make you feel welcome in a new school?

_____

_____

_____

_____

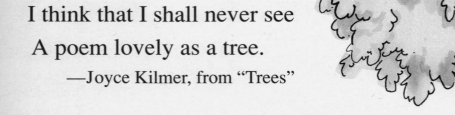

Trees

I think that I shall never see
A poem lovely as a tree.

—Joyce Kilmer, from "Trees"

Do you think that a tree is one of the prettiest things
in the world? Tell why or why not.

_____

_____

_____

What does a tree make you think of? What colors?
What sounds? What animals? Make lists.

Colors	Sounds	Animals
_____	_____	_____
_____	_____	_____
_____	_____	_____

 DURING READING

Read "Begin at the Beginning." Learn what a
tree means to a girl named Sara.

Three Beginnings

Pretend that Sara's teacher asks her to write a story about her tree. Sara writes three beginnings. She can't decide which one to use. Read the three beginnings. Put a ✔ in the 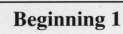 that goes with the one you like best. Then write what happens next.

Beginning 1

One day a squirrel came to my tree carrying a nut. The squirrel dropped the nut into a hole in my tree.

Beginning 2

I fell asleep under my tree one summer afternoon. When I opened my eyes, a rabbit spoke to me. "Play with me," it said.

Beginning 3

A bird flew into my tree and started building a nest.

_____

_____

_____

_____

_____

_____

_____

_____

The STRANGE Bird

Imagine that a strange bird flew into Sara's tree while she was looking out the window. What did the bird look like? Its head and its claws are on this page. Draw and color the rest of the strange bird.

Name your bird.

Why did the bird land in Sara's tree? What did the bird see and do while it was there? Did any other animals come by? Pretend that you are the bird. Write about the time you spent in Sara's tree.

Show your picture and story to a friend. Look at your friend's picture and story. Talk about how they are alike and how they are not alike.

Bits and Pieces

Imagine you found a trunk full of cloth—all
bits and pieces. What would you make from
the pieces of cloth? A rag rug? A quilt? A tent?
A dress? A jacket? Think up lots of ideas.
Then draw the one thing you would make.
Use different colors to show the pieces.

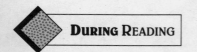 **DURING READING**

Read the next story, "Harlequin and the Gift of
Many Colors." Find out what a boy named
Harlequin makes from bits of old cloth.

CARNIVAL TIME

Have you ever been to a carnival or a fair? Make a list of some things that you might see at a carnival or a fair.

What kinds of foods could you eat at a carnival or a fair?

_____

_____

_____

_____

_____

_____

_____

_____

Write about a visit to a carnival or a fair. It can be a real carnival. It can be like the carnival that Harlequin went to, or it can be a make-believe carnival.

_____

_____

_____

_____

_____

_____

_____

_____

_____

ANOTHER HARLEQUIN

Paulo as Harlequin, Pablo Picasso, 1924

In some plays, a harlequin is a kind of clown. He usually wears a mask and a costume with many colors. This is a famous painting by Pablo Picasso. Picasso painted his son Paulo dressed as a harlequin. How old do you think Paulo is in the painting?

_____

Draw and color your own harlequin. Give
your clown a face, a costume, and a name.

Color in the face that shows how much you liked each story, article, or poem in this unit.

Draw a line under the name of your favorite story, article, or poem. Circle the one you liked least.

On what page in your Reader's Journal do you think you did your best work for this unit? Why do you think so?

Too Many Babas

Helping

Check It Out!

Nick Joins In

Begin at the Beginning

Harlequin and the Gift of Many Colors

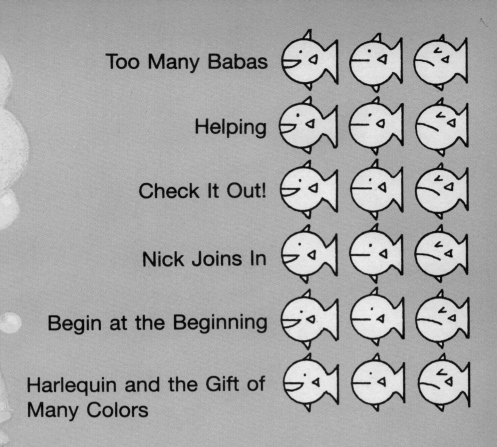

Choose what you want to do.

What's For Lunch?

Make a small box for soup and sandwich recipes. Put some blank cards inside. Ask your friends to help you write good recipes on the cards.

Harlequin Hat

Make a harlequin hat. Color two big pieces of white paper. Hold the two pieces of paper together and cut one harlequin hat shape. Tape the sides together.

Puppet Time

With your class, make puppets out of small paper bags. Make one puppet a clown. Have a puppet show outside at recess.

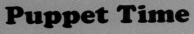

I Can Help

Write a list of ways you could help people. Then make a "Good Deeds" chart. Give yourself a star for every time you help someone.

NEW WORDS I'VE LEARNED

_____   _____
_____   _____
_____   _____
_____   _____
_____   _____
_____   _____

WORDS TO LEARN TO SPELL

_____   _____
_____   _____
_____   _____
_____   _____
_____   _____

BOOKS I'VE READ

_____

_____

_____

_____

_____

_____

_____

_____

_____

_____

_____

_____

BOOKS I'D LIKE TO READ

_____

_____

_____

_____

_____

_____

_____

_____

_____

_____

_____

A B C D E F G H I J - GB - 96 95 94 93 92 91 90